Special Needs Education:
Navigating for Your Child

To my late father, who was visually impaired and never received the benefits of special education in the 1930s and 1940s.

Parker Press Inc.
Briarcliff Manor, NY 10510

ISBN: 978-1-941760-04-8

For the latest information and updates to this material, check out:
http://www.reallifelegal.com/updates

Special Needs Education:
Navigating for Your Child

Lynne Williams, Esq.

Real Life Legal™

Helpful Guides for Everyday Legal Matters

Parker Press Inc.

Contents

Contents

What This Book's About

Whether your child has just been diagnosed with a disability, you are dissatisfied with the special education received or you want to be sure your child is receiving all benefits to which he or she is entitled, this book can help you.

Many parents have walked in your shoes and this book shares the wisdom learned as you set about understanding what the law requires when it comes to educating a special needs child. As with many government and administrative "entitlements," perseverance pays. You'll learn from trial and error. This book aims to help you get through the trials and avoid the errors.

Depending on your child's condition or illness, you may have already been on quite a journey getting to the point of confirming a diagnosis. As a nation, we are experiencing alarming rates of new or expanding special needs conditions such as autism, ADD and ADHD. But parents whose children have disabilities have been fighting for their child's needs for years.

Once children have been diagnosed with a disability, federal laws entitle them to a public education that meets certain standards. It's up to parents to make sure their special needs children get the education the law entitles them to. Without parents' advocacy, delivery on education for disabled students can fall short.

Facing a Special Needs Diagnosis

If you are the parent or guardian of a child recently diagnosed with a disability, you may be consumed with sadness, grief, anger or despair. Make sure you connect with others in the community who have had similar experiences. There are many resources, including hospitals, state agencies and nonprofit organizations that sponsor support groups for parents of children with specific disabilities. Don't wait to seek them out, as they will be a great source of support for you. Don't make the mistake of sacrificing your own well-being to pursue your desire to do what is necessary for your child.

Children Newly Diagnosed with Special Needs

If your child has recently been diagnosed with a disability, you are probably trying to learn everything you can about the disability and how best to help and support your child. For infant children, with a new diagnosis, there is some time, but not much.

It's good to start early in understanding the childhood education process for young children with disabilities. If your child is school age, or even preschool age, time is of the essence!

Understanding your child's rights and ensuring his or her education is properly addressed by your school district is a fundamental mission of a parent or guardian of a special needs child. How the education is delivered, and making sure it in fact happens in the way it should, may require rigorous participation by parents of special needs children. Parents must take action if those rights are violated. Parents of special needs children cannot be on auto-pilot when it comes to their child's education.

Children Receiving Special Needs Services

If your child is currently receiving special education services or has already been diagnosed with a disability requiring such services, this book can help if you are:

- Dissatisfied with the services (either the type of services being provided or the manner in which they are being provided).

- The school district has failed to fully provide the agreed-upon services.

Even if you know and understand the basic legal and regulatory underpinnings of special education, this book will likely add a real life dimension. Presented are various remedies, both informal and formal, available to the parents or guardians who seek to ensure that their children are receiving the services to which they are entitled.

Special Needs Education Beyond High School

If you are the parent or guardian of a child who will soon be transitioning out of high school, you may be at a loss as to how to support that transition. This book addresses the issue of transitional services for students receiving special education. You'll understand what is mandated by law as well as gain insight into those services that, while not mandated, are certainly worth arguing for, on behalf of your child.

Special Needs Advocacy: Do You Need a Lawyer?

Often the parents or guardians of a special needs child do what it takes to get the best education for their child. But if you're in a tough situation and the school district isn't responsive, hiring a lawyer may make sense.

In order to ensure special needs children get what they are entitled to, parents or guardians do the legwork with the school district to get the job done. Depending on your situation, you may need a lawyer to protect and assert your child's rights.

For example, there may be times in this process you choose to challenge a decision made by the school district, either through an administrative proceeding or in federal court. The goal of this book is to show how things work. It does not offer legal advice or replace the services of a lawyer, if needed.

Contact Your State's Parent Information and Training Center

Every state has a center which provides information and training to parents and guardians of children with disabilities, to enable them to participate more fully with the educators and professionals working with their children.

Make sure you contact your state's parent and information training center early on at: http://www.parentcenterhub.org/find-your-center/

Finding an Attorney for Special Needs Education

Most state departments of education provide a list of attorneys experienced in special education law. Some private attorneys are willing to significantly reduce their fees for **"Due Process Hearing"** representation (discussed on page 42) because if you prevail, and/or go to federal court, attorney's fees may be awarded.

Many nonprofit agencies have staff attorneys who may also be able to help. However, because of funding constraints, these nonprofits may limit their cases to students with specific disabilities. On the plus side, if your child fits into an area of their advocacy, they may take your child's case and represent you at no cost.

It is also possible to retain a non-attorney (lay) advocate to assist you in pursuing a due process hearing, but be aware that you cannot be reimbursed for the advocate's fees. Also be aware that a parent, who is an attorney, cannot be reimbursed for time spent on his or her child's case.

Federal Law Mandates Education for the Disabled

Federal law mandates that individuals with disabilities receive a public education that takes into account their special needs. States implement these programs and may have rules of their own.

The major law in providing education for the disabled is a federal law known as the **"Individuals with Disabilities Education Act (IDEA)."** Enacted in 1975, IDEA mandates that states provide special education for those with disabilities. It was enacted to address the failure of state education systems to educate students with disabilities. While all states currently have their own laws and regulations concerning special education, they must all adhere to the basic protections of the IDEA.

State Resources for Educating the Disabled

Go online to your state's department of education website, search for your state's special education laws and regulations and download. Your state may provide some services and protections over and above what the IDEA requires. Be aware, too, that these laws change frequently, so review them for updates every year.

States can pass laws and regulations that give greater services and protections to students with disabilities than the IDEA affords, but they cannot give less than what the federal law requires.

What Is a Regulation?

A **"regulation"** is an administrative rule enacted by a federal, or state, agency that is designed to implement a law. For example, the IDEA is very broad and general and does not address the specifics of implementation. That's where federal and state regulations come in. Federal regulations are found in what is known as the **"Code of Federal Regulations (CFR)"** and each state also has its own regulations.

Many federal laws (e.g., Medicare and Medicaid) spell out general requirements, but the specifics of implementation are left up to the states. The regulations spell out the details about how the states will bring the law into action within their jurisdiction. Regulations cover the administrative specifics, rather than the "entitlement" that is mandated by federal law. They provide the rules of the road for getting benefits in the state as required by federal mandates.

If you want to gain a deeper understanding of how things work, read the regulations your state adopted to follow the IDEA. The IDEA itself will not be particularly helpful to read.

Practical Advice About Regulations

If you do not understand an aspect of any law or regulation pertaining to special education, do not hesitate to call the special education department of your state department of education. There is almost always someone in the department who can explain the law and regulations to you in plain language.

Your Child's Rights and the IDEA

Whether your child is entitled to a special education program depends on professional evaluations in alignment with the IDEA and regulations.

The first step in determining whether your child is eligible for special education is based on the results of one or more evaluations, which are reviewed by a team of professionals. The testing plan is generally determined by the child's age, what the deficits appear to be and any prior diagnoses received. It also includes testing, observation and reporting from parents and school personnel.

Evaluating Special Needs

Testing and evaluation are the key ingredients of a special needs determination. These may include:

- Cognitive testing.
- Skills testing, in subjects such as reading or math.
- Psychological testing.
- Speech evaluations.
- Behavioral testing.

All children are entitled by law to receive a **"free, appropriate public education (FAPE)."** That is the standard used in the context of disabled children. For example, if your child has a physical disability, but that disability does not require any special services or accommodations to enable him or her to receive FAPE, he or she will likely not be eligible for special education services.

Disabilities That Warrant Special Education Services

Most commonly known disabilities will enable your child to qualify for special education services. Yet merely having the disability is not enough without a showing that the services are needed. Not all those with disabilities require special services.

Under the IDEA, the following disability categories are indicators of eligibility for special education services: autism, deafness, deaf-blindness, hearing impairment, mental retardation, multiple disabilities, orthopedic impairment, other health impairment, serious emotional disturbance, specific learning disability, speech or language impairment, traumatic brain injury and visual impairment, including blindness. The IDEA list is not exclusive and is augmented by "degrees of disability," other "health impairments" and new conditions that change the law.

Supplementing the list of disabilities in the IDEA are many sub-categories of disabilities. For example, Asperger's is a sub-category of autism, stuttering is a sub-category of speech or language impairment, and there are many sub-categories that *may* fall under serious emotional disturbances, such as obsessive-compulsive disorder, oppositional-defiant disorder or bipolar disorder. Also, keep in mind that many of these disorders range from mild to severe and eligibility is determined by severity and impact on educational benefit.

Other Health Impairments Treated as Disabilities

"Other Health Impaired (OHI)" is a catchall category that includes disabilities that don't fit into any of the other categories. For example, Attention Deficit and Attention Deficit Hyperactivity Disorders (ADD and ADHD, respectively) fall into this category, unless combined with another disorder that has its own category. Even so, the student would likely be found eligible, if he or she is found to be eligible, under the categorized disability. Many physical disabilities (e.g., cerebral palsy and spina bifida) also fall under OHI.

Special Education Disabilities

- Autism
- Deaf-blindness
- Hearing impairment
- Mental retardation
- Multiple disabilities
- Orthopedic impairment
- Serious emotional disturbance
- Learning disabilities
- Speech or language impairment
- Traumatic brain injury
- Visual impairment or blindness
- Obsessive-compulsive disorder
- Bipolar disorder
- Asperger's
- ADD, ADHD, cerebral palsy, etc.

It may come as a surprise, but just because your child has a disability, he or she is not automatically qualified for special education services. Such services must be necessary in order to ensure that he or she receives a free, appropriate public education or FAPE.

Eligibility vs. Accommodations for Special Needs Students

There are times when a student is deemed "not eligible" for special education services but needs certain accommodations in order to access his education. Accommodations are not governed by the IDEA. Instead they fall under Section 504 of the **"Federal Rehabilitation Act."**

Passed in 1973, this Act is considered the first national declaration of the rights of people with disabilities. It prohibits recipients of any type of federal funding (such as school districts) from discriminating on the basis of disability. This law protects people with disabilities in many aspects of life, including education.

If your child does not qualify for services under the IDEA, but has specific needs that require accommodations, it is imperative that you request that he or she be considered for accommodations under Section 504. Accommodations can include:

- Academic modifications, including increasing testing times.

- Reducing homework assignments.

- Allowing the use of a note taker or taped lectures.

- Physical accommodations, such as preferential seating.

- Installation of restroom grab bars or other modifications to the physical plant.

- Provision of a one-on-one aide during the school day, whether for academic, behavior, health or accessibility reasons.

REAL LIFE EXAMPLE

Amy, who is in the 4th grade, has visual impairments, and is struggling in her math class. Her teacher referred her for special education services and various assessments were completed. Amy's cognitive assessment shows her to be above average in cognitive ability, and the academic assessments show her capability to be average or above, including in math. The team contacts her ophthalmologist and asks for a report on Amy's visual acuity. A review of this report suggests that Amy is having difficulty seeing the whiteboard, which her teacher uses throughout the class.

It is determined that Amy does not require direct special education services in order to make educational progress, but that she does need preferential seating in the first row of the classroom (or even closer to the board if need be) in order for her to receive a "free, appropriate public education." A two-month check-in by the team indicates that Amy is now making average progress in her math class, owing to the accommodations that were made.

Even though these types of accommodations are not governed by the IDEA, and instead fall under Section 504 of the Federal Rehabilitation Act, they must be considered as part of an "individual education plan" or IEP for a student who is eligible for special education services.

Formulating an Individual Education Plan (IEP)

Federal law requires the school district to come up with a plan just for your child. The plan is the cornerstone to your child's special education services.

Your child's educational needs are addressed by a school district through an **"Individualized Education Plan (IEP)."** An IEP "team" is the decision-making body regarding your child's education (at least at the beginning of the process).

What is the Individualized Education Plan (IEP)?

The IEP is a road map, detailing the services and accommodations, if necessary, that will enable your child to make educational progress. The IEP will typically include direct educational services, ancillary services (e.g., speech therapy or counseling) and accommodations, such as preferential seating, reduced homework or testing modifications. It is the IEP team that hammers out the details of the IEP, usually with input from the professionals involved in providing the services and sometimes with input from independent professionals.

IEP at Home

An IEP *does not* address issues that occur in the home. Issues around home-based situations such as homework non-performance and other behavioral issues relative to school or schoolwork, are not the concern of the school. For example, if homework is not submitted because of stress at home, a student will not be exempt from his academic obligations. That said, however, the IEP team is empowered to review and modify the homework, testing and other performance obligations of the student, after review of his or her disability and particular needs.

For example, students with certain disabilities, such as Attention Deficit Disorder (ADD), Attention Deficit Hyperactivity Disorder (ADHD), learning disabilities, autism and various other disabilities, will frequently struggle with homework assignments.

It is your responsibility to convince the team that your child is not a slacker, a manipulator or a malingerer (common adjectives heard used by school personnel in this context). It may involve demonstrating that when the student is given a reasonable amount of homework, it is done well and submitted on time. However, it may take a private professional assessment and an expert opinion that argues that there should be homework and/or testing accommodations.

The IEP Team

There are certain individuals who must, by law, be members of the IEP team. First and foremost are the parents or guardians of the student. The parents or guardians have first-hand experience with the students and likely possess invaluable insight into their needs and how they can best be satisfied in the educational environment.

The team must include an administrator who has the authority to make financial or budgetary decisions, which is essentially the authority to commit district funds. This legal requirement avoids the necessity that team decisions be reviewed by another entity. This role is often, although not always, filled by the district's director of special education, or a person with a similar title. Sometimes, however, a school principal or vice-principal will take on this role.

Other team members almost always include the student's current teacher, whether or not the child is currently placed in a special education classroom, and any professionals providing special education services outside of the classroom. Also integral to the team are any therapists providing services to the student, most notably speech therapists, occupational therapists and physical therapists.

IEP Team Members

- Parents or guardians.
- District financial administrator.
- Teachers.
- Guidance counselors.
- Therapists involved with the student.
- Student (if possible).
- Medical professionals.

For students receiving counseling or psychological support services, the counselor should be included as part of the team. Likewise, if the student has medical issues, a doctor or other medical professional may be part of the team. Frequently the input from the therapists, counselors and medical professionals is in the form of written reports rather than appearances at team meetings.

The student always has a right to participate in the team meetings. Obviously this would depend on the age of the child and the severity of the disability, and it is the parents' or guardians' decision to make. If the students are eighteen or older, they must either participate or designate in writing who will represent their interests at the team meeting. If a parent or guardian has guardianship of a student eighteen or older, he or she would serve as the student's representative at the team meeting.

You, as a parent or guardian, must educate yourself about the process, the law and the regulations if you are to participate as an equal IEP team member on behalf of your child.

How the IEP Team Makes Decisions

The team decides whether your child is eligible for special education based on the results of one or more professional evaluations. By way of examples, the evaluation process may include cognitive testing, skills testing (e.g., reading, math and other topic areas), psychological testing, speech evaluations, behavioral testing, classroom observations and reporting from parents and school personnel. The testing plan is determined by the child's age, what his or her deficits appear to be and any prior diagnoses received.

Challenging a Special Needs Assessment

At times the family, as members of the team, may be concerned about the reliability of a given assessment or the objectivity or, rarely, the competency of an evaluator. The family has the right to request an independent evaluation.

This evaluation is done by an independent professional who is not: (1) a school district employee or (2) a current contractor employed by the school district.

However, the school district may stand by the appropriateness of the evaluation that was already done and refuse to order an independent evaluation. The family then typically has two options: (1) pay for an independent evaluation or (2) file for a due process hearing (discussed on page 42). This is an opportunity to argue that the school district has the responsibility to order and pay for an independent evaluation.

If an independent evaluation is completed, regardless of whether at the parents' or the district's expense, the team must consider it as part of the discussion regarding eligibility and services.

Attorney at the IEP Team Meeting

Typically you do not need an attorney to represent you at a team meeting, and if you do bring an attorney, the school has the right to have the school district's attorney present. Having attorneys present at IEP team meetings, particularly at the early stages of the process, is not conducive to coming to consensus on a plan for your child. That said, however, your emotional involvement with your child sometimes can result in an inability to engage in an objective debate about what educational services will be right for him.

As the parent of a child with disabilities, Rose always brought someone to accompany her to team meetings. She brought either another parent or an advocate from a program working with children with disabilities. Rose found that because of the emotions that always welled up when anyone was discussing her child, she was better able to protect her child's interests by stepping back and letting another advocate speak for her if she felt it was necessary. The presence of another person, who is not a lawyer, helped Rose better advocate for her child.

How Special Needs Diagnoses Can Result in Different Treatment

There are a number of reasons why two children with the same diagnosed disability might have different special education eligibility status.

Becky and Bobby both have language-based learning disabilities and both are in the third grade. Both students' assessments included reading tests and cognitive ability testing. Bobby's testing indicated that, relevant to his cognitive ability, and despite his learning disability, he is reading at or near the appropriate level. The team decides that Bobby does not need special education services, but that some classroom support, from an aide already working in the classroom, would help Bobby reach grade level in reading.

Becky's scores show that relative to her cognitive level, she is reading significantly below what might be expected, and the team decides that she requires direct special education services to address her learning disability. However, both teams agree to reconvene at the start of the next term, or before if indicated, to reassess whether progress is in fact occurring for both children.

Keep in mind that there are two elements of eligibility for special needs education: an eligible disability and the need for special education services in order to make educational progress in school.

Extracurricular Activities

Most schools give access to extracurricular activities to students with disabilities on the same basis that non-disabled students are given access. For example, if team membership requires a certain level of athletic skill, that level must be met regardless of disability. That said however, many extracurricular activities can be accessible to students with disabilities if they are given some aids and supports.

Extracurricular activities can enhance your child's school experience, and the IDEA and Section 504 require that all students be given access to extracurricular activities.

Under a 2010 court ruling, the IDEA requires school districts to offer students with disabilities an equal opportunity to participate in extracurricular activities. The IEP team determines what activities are appropriate for the student, and incorporates them into the IEP. These activities are not limited to activities that "educate the child." It is important that you, as the parent or guardian, raise the issue of extracurricular activities at team meetings, and advocate for your child to participate in them. This may mean arguing that aids and supports are provided to make it possible for the child to participate in such activities.

When it comes to providing aid and support, think broadly as to how this can be achieved. For example, support could include modifying a part in a play so that a student who utilizes a wheelchair can play a certain role. Or it could take the form of providing a runner/aide so that a blind student can join the track team. Even simply instructing members of a club that they must always face a hearing impaired student when they are speaking, so that he can understand what they are saying, can constitute aid and support.

REAL LIFE EXAMPLE

Sandy has cerebral palsy and has difficulty using the neighborhood playground, even with assistance. She attends an after-school program at the local YMCA where she is included in activities with non-disabled children. She gets help with homework, does arts and crafts and science activities and takes nature walks. She also participates in social skills groups, where she serves as a group leader and is learning to develop her leadership skills.

Many public and private recreation areas, from state parks to private ski resorts, provide programing for those with disabilities, both youths and adults. In addition, the Special Olympics provide opportunities to engage in sports activities. A few years ago, a blind hiker hiked the entire Appalachian Trail, along with his seeing-eye dog.

Examples of Non-academic Services and Extracurricular Activities

- School newspaper and literary journals.

- Sports.

- Chorus.

- Band.

- Theater.

- Special interest groups and clubs.

Legal Remedies for a Failed IEP

If the IEP created for your child is not working, carefully consider why it's failing and seek to resolve the problem at that point. Escalating concerns up a chain of command can escalate the problem and make resolution more difficult.

When an IEP is not working well, address the issue first with the school district personnel closest to the problem. There is often a higher degree of success by starting at this level, rather than taking it to the "top" and alienating all layers of administration in between. For example, if the problem is a teacher who is not implementing her part of the IEP, having a meeting with that teacher, and exploring the aspects of the plan that are not being implemented, could resolve the problem. Certainly, you will meet less pushback than if you contacted her superior to complain, so it is worth a try to start at the lowest point in the chain of command to resolve the problem.

What do you do if your student has an IEP that you consider inadequate or not being fully implemented? The first step is to request an informal meeting with the appropriate school personnel.

If you fail to get results at the initial level, move up the chain of supervision, even if it means risking resistance from the teacher or therapist. This risk is one worth taking because at the least, by communicating within the chain of supervision at the school, you demonstrate trying to work things out. These communication efforts may be very important evidence of your good faith if you're later forced into an administrative hearing.

If informal conversations with the relevant personnel do not bear fruit, request an IEP meeting, so that the entire team can consider your concerns. Give thought to what you can produce to substantiate your concern. While a parent's concern with an IEP, or its implementation, warrants an IEP meeting, you're more likely to be successful in making your case if you have professional support.

Sara, a disabled child, has an independent counselor who believes that Sara's classroom teacher is not implementing the IEP, because the teacher does not allow Sara a "time out" when she becomes emotionally stressed. Sara's parents will have far more influence at the IEP meeting if they can bring a statement or a report from the counselor. When the counselor states that there is a failure to fully implement the IEP, such that there is a negative impact on Sara's receipt of a free, appropriate public education, it carries more weight than if the parents show up and just state this is happening.

To the extent that aspects of the IEP are clear, you will need little professional support. For example, if the IEP specifies a limit on the amount of homework, and that limit is not being respected, professional support may not be needed. Instead, it will not be difficult for you to ask that the team to explain why the IEP is not being implemented and then demand that it be properly implemented. Keep in mind that it is not your responsibility to explain why the amount of homework is being limited; that ground was ploughed when that IEP team decision was incorporated into the IEP.

Failure to Address IEP Issues

If, following one or more IEP meetings, the team fails to address what you consider to be either non-implementation of the IEP or an inadequate IEP, the next step will take place at the administrative level. The law requires your state's department of education to offer mediation in an attempt to resolve your dispute with the school district. It is essential to understand just what mediation is, and is not, before you decide to go this route.

Attorneys in Mediation

Having attorneys present at mediation may not be the best way to go for several reasons. For starters, attorneys are trained to rely on the law and legal argument, often in a confrontational manner. Mediators, on the other hand, are trained to facilitate consensus, with the goal of leading parties to a mutually acceptable agreement. The law is often a win-lose proposition; mediation tries to be win-win. However, if the mediation produces a "draft agreement," you should have it reviewed by your attorney, or advocate, if you have one.

Mediation by the State Department of Education

Mediation is a voluntary process, and can be a good opportunity to make your case. If discussions with the school district have become frustrating or even confrontational, mediation will allow an independent professional to facilitate dialogue that will, hopefully, lead to an agreement. Here are some pointers on mediation:

- You cannot be forced or required to engage in mediation with the school district.

- It is very important to the process that both parties, you and the school district's representative, mediate in good faith, with the goal of resolving the dispute.

- Mediation involves no cost to the parties.

When Mediation Doesn't Work

If mediation doesn't work, you are entitled to a due process hearing. This is a formal process, wherein an independent hearing officer will hear testimony about your matter and issue a legally defensible opinion.

At a due process hearing, it is a good idea to have an attorney, since it is rare that a non-represented person can prevail.

A "**due process hearing**" is an administrative hearing presided over by an independent hearing officer. The IDEA gives all parents and guardians of students covered under the IDEA the right to a due process hearing. Adult students (age eighteen to twenty-three) with disabilities have the same right.

A due process hearing, like other types of administrative hearings, does not stick to the letter of the law when it comes to the rules of evidence. For example, in a typical court room case, testimony of those not present (known as hearsay) often cannot be presented to make a case. With a due process hearing, the evidentiary rules are relaxed. However the administrative hearing process is still a formal process which means that:

- Witnesses testify under oath.

- A court reporter takes down the proceedings.

- All witnesses can be cross-examined by opposing counsel.

While any administrative or judicial proceedings are pending, the school district is not permitted to change the placement of the student. This provision is called "stay put," and is designed to prevent arbitrary changes to the student's IEP during the time that the hearing officer or a judge is weighing the issues in the matter. A change of location where services are provided is not considered a change in placement, as long as the substance of the IEP continues to be provided in the least restrictive alternative. However, if the family and the district mutually agree to a change in program, it is permissible.

Due Process Hearing: Don't Go It Alone

Even if you have learned everything that you can about special education law, it is rare that a lay person can navigate a due process hearing without counsel. A due process hearing often involves the drafting and submission of pre-hearing memoranda and post-hearing briefs. It's important to have an attorney experienced in these matters on your team at this stage of the process.

Time Limit on IEP Issues

Under current federal law, you must raise a legal issue regarding your child's education within two years of identifying the issue. So, if you note that there are problems with implementation of your child's IEP, you must raise the issues within two years, which parents usually do. However, this time frame also means that you cannot reach back more than two years to make your case.

The parents of Bradley, a special needs child, have complained that the school district has repeatedly failed to provide the amount of hours of speech therapy that Bradley's IEP specifies. The parents' complaints go back three years. However, because of the two-year legal requirement, Bradley's parents cannot use evidence from three years ago to bolster their case.

There is essentially a two-year **"statute of limitations"** on raising issues about your child's IEP. If there is a problem with the IEP, raise the issues quickly. It becomes too late to: (1) raise concerns if two years elapse, and (2) offer substantiation about the failed plan for activities which occurred more than two years before being challenged.

Winning a Due Process Hearing

At some point in your child's educational process, you may end up filing for a due process hearing. In a special education due process hearing, you have to convince the hearing officer that the allegations in your complaint are true and that the remedies you seek are appropriate. In other words, you have the "burden of proof" to show this. While you will likely have an attorney represent you, your record keeping and preparation will be critical to your success.

There are a broad range of remedies that the hearing officer can award a prevailing family, depending on the issues raised at the hearing. If those issues included a failure to provide FAPE for a period of time, the hearing officer could order compensatory education. This would consist of additional services over and above what is ordered in the IEP. If the student's day is already filled up, these services could be delivered during the summer and other vacation periods or after school.

Keep Good Records

Preparation for a due process hearing starts long before you may even know what a hearing is. To prove your case it is essential to have good records.

- Keep every document regarding your child's education, all reports, all parent-school communications, report cards, parent-teacher diaries, any and everything.

- Make audio tapes of IEP meetings, as is your right.

- Make and keep notes of telephone conversations with school personnel and retain all emails.

- Make notes of complaints and positive comments made by your child regarding his or her school experience.

The hearing officer can also order a different placement. This can mean placement in a different classroom or a different school, including a residential placement, if the hearing officer determines that the current placement does not deliver FAPE to the student. Other remedies can include:

- Ordering the school district to begin delivering necessary services that the team failed to order.

- Reimbursing the family for an independent evaluation that the district would not fund, but which the hearing officer determined was necessary.

- Fully implementing an IEP in place, if it is found to be appropriate and was not properly implemented.

- Adjusting the IEP so that it is appropriate and designed to deliver FAPE.

- Issuing an order to remedy the situation.

Losing the Due Process Hearing

If the Due Process Hearing officer finds against you, you have two options: Appeal the decision to the Federal District Court, or take advantage of a state process to investigate your complaint.

Appealing to Federal Court

Since the IDEA is a federal law, cases which contest the findings of an administrative hearing are brought to federal court with jurisdiction over your state, or the area of your state where your child attends school. While going to federal court may seem like a daunting alternative, depending on what's at stake and your chances of success (based on court decisions in your area), it may be worth pursuing. Keep in mind that a federal court case:

- Is much more complicated than the due process hearing.

- Definitely requires hiring an attorney to represent you.

- Requires some research beforehand to determine your likelihood of success.

Many federal special education decisions are posted online. If you're considering an appeal of a due process finding to federal court, check the decisions in the federal court jurisdiction that would handle your appeal. You want to get an idea of your likelihood of success with the issues you've raised. For example, if you are pushing for a certain type of one-on-one aide to support your child in extracurricular activities, and the federal court which oversees your jurisdiction has repeatedly ruled that a FAPE does not require the type of one-on-one support you seek, it may not be worthwhile to pursue.

Seeking State Remedies After Losing a Due Process Hearing

States are also required to offer a complaint investigation process, which is undertaken by investigators employed by the state. The investigator presents findings to the Commissioner of Education, who then determines whether a violation of law under the IDEA or state special education law has occurred. If it is found that a violation has occurred, a corrective action plan will be developed and implemented.

State complaint investigations are most effective when there are suspected systemic violations, such as the district's refusal to find eligibility based on certain disabilities, or a district's failure to provide related services, such as speech therapy. State investigations are generally less effective when dealing with implementation of one student's IEP.

Special Education for Preschool Children

If you know your child will need special education, it's not too early to make inquires. Programs are available for infants and preschoolers.

Preschool children fall into two categories: birth to age three and age three to age five. From birth to age three, children who are eligible can receive what are known as "early intervention" services. Under the IDEA, children from age three to age five with disabilities must receive special education services through "Pre-K" programs.

What is Early Intervention?

"Early intervention" is the process by which young children, already identified with a physical or mental condition that has a high probability of causing, or having caused, a developmental delay, are provided services. These services must also be provided to children who are otherwise at risk of developing a special need that will negatively impact their education.

_____

Early intervention services, for preschool–age children, can be in any, or all, of five developmental areas: physical development, cognitive development, social and/or emotional development, adaptive development and communication.

_____

The IDEA requires that the needs of the child receiving early intervention services must be addressed in natural environments to the maximum extent possible. A natural environment is one in which a non-disabled child in a similar age range would be placed. This is not just a preference but a legal requirement.

Brandon was born with multiple physical birth defects and spent six months in a neonatal unit in a hospital. Upon release, he showed significant developmental delays. He was placed in a regular infant childcare center and a physical therapist and an occupational therapist each visited three times a week to provide his therapy. The IDEA mandates that Brandon receive this type of care.

Determining Eligibility for Early Intervention Services

The multi-disciplinary early intervention team is composed of qualified professionals in the areas of physical development, hearing and vision, speech and language and other developmental areas. These professionals perform specialized testing as well as observe and interact with your child, to assess how your child functions and whether he or she has reached appropriate developmental milestones. Parents and guardians are also an integral part of the team.

If your child is determined to be eligible, the team will schedule a team meeting to develop an **"Individualized Family Service Plan (IFSP)."** The IFSP contains a description of the services that are necessary to assist children with their developmental challenges.

Length of Eligibility

The team will begin to prepare the child for transition to special education services around the age of thirty months and final transition should occur at thirty-six months. Even if your child was eligible for, and received, early intervention services, there is no guarantee that he or she will be eligible for preschool special education services. A transition-planning meeting will be held to discuss next steps, which may include updated, or new, assessments and services to assist your child with the transition process. An exit IEP is developed, which describes the services and supports your child will receive after the transition.

Transitioning out of Early Child Education Services into a Pre-K Program

All preschool-age children with disabilities, as enumerated in the IDEA, must be provided free and appropriate Pre-K programs. In addition, those children who continue to manifest developmental delays, even if not specifically identified with a disability under the IDEA, must continue to be provided with Pre-K services. These delays must be in one or more of these areas:

- Physical development.

- Cognitive development.

- Communication development.

- Social or emotional development.

- Adaptive development.

As with school-age children with disabilities, Pre-K children have the right to FAPE in the "**least restrictive environment**." This mandate requires that those children with disabilities must receive their education alongside children without disabilities to the maximum extent possible.

A district may provide Pre-K services in a district-run early education program, such as a community-based "Head Start" program, or in a private Pre-K program.

The IEP that was developed when the student transitioned out of early intervention services will specify the services that the child will receive when placed in the Pre-K program. The IEP must include a statement of how the child's disability will affect his participation in age-appropriate Pre-K activities, as well as any supplementary aids and services necessary to meet his or her unique needs. For example, an IEP may provide that the child receive an assistive technology device, a sign-language interpreter or bathroom modifications. The IEP team is also required to discuss and provide necessary program modifications and supports for school personnel, such as specialized training.

Under the IDEA, a child's placement in a segregated classroom or program cannot occur except when the nature or severity of the child's disability is such that education in regular classes cannot be achieved satisfactorily.

REAL LIFE EXAMPLE

Matt suffered a traumatic brain injury at birth. He is now four years old and not yet toilet trained. The school district is required to provide an aide at his Head Start program to assist him with toileting. This aide also assists another little boy in the same program with utilizing an adaptive communication device and a third child with navigating the Head Start facility in his wheelchair.

IEP Timelines, Timeframes and Deadlines

As with many things in the law, the IDEA includes deadlines and time frames for voicing concerns and problems and for the district's responsibility to provide notice and share information. Know the rules and be sure they are working in your favor.

The IDEA mandates certain deadlines for notice, assessments, and development and implementation of the IEP. States can impose shorter deadlines to facilitate and expedite the process, but they cannot delay the process with longer deadlines than the IDEA mandates. Following are examples of IDEA deadlines:

- Ten days in advance of an IEP meeting, you must be provided with a written notice of the meeting and the reason for the meeting.

- Upon initial referral for special education services, and thereafter once a year, the school district is required to provide the parents or guardian with a copy of the Procedural Safeguards. **"Procedural Safeguards"** is a statement that lists the family's rights under the IDEA. These include the right to be on the team and get notice of all meetings, provide written consent (or not) to assessments, mediation, a due process hearing and free services.

- You must also be given a copy when you file a complaint with the state or a request for a due process hearing.

- The IEP team shall complete the initial assessment of your child and determine eligibility within sixty calendar days of receiving your consent for the assessments and within ninety calendar days of receiving a written referral for an assessment.

- The IEP must be developed within thirty calendar days of the date of determination of eligibility. It must be implemented as soon as possible after it is developed, unless the team meeting is held during summer break or a school vacation period. It must then be implemented immediately when school commences, with the exception of those services that may take some extra time to arrange (e.g., hiring a sign-language interpreter or establishing transportation).

- The IEP team must meet to develop, review and, if necessary, revise your child's IEP at least annually, and more frequently if necessary.

- The IEP team must conduct a reevaluation of your child's eligibility for special education and related services at least once every three years. If the team determines that updated data is needed, the relevant assessments must be conducted, and the report(s) completed within ninety calendar days of the team meeting at which they were ordered.

The IEP team also determines whether your child requires **"extended school year (ESY)"** services and this determination must be made at least annually. ESY services are required when it is predicted that there will be significant regression of the progress made by the student if he or she is without certain services during the summer or school vacations.

REAL LIFE EXAMPLE

Ross is a six-year old who has been diagnosed with autism. With the help of a one-on-one aide who is skilled in teaching children with autism, Ross made excellent progress during the first term of his first grade year. However, when he returned to school after the winter break, he had already lost many of his new skills. While he made additional progress during the beginning of the year, Ross again regressed during the spring break. The IEP team met in April to determine whether Ross needed ESY during the summer. The team determined that Ross's regression during the winter and the spring breaks provided sufficient evidence that he was at risk for regression without ESY services. Accordingly, such services are added to his IEP.

The meeting to determine a child's need for ESY services should be conducted early enough in the school year to provide the parent with an opportunity to request mediation or file a due process complaint if the district does not agree to an ESY.

Special Education in Special Circumstances

Special education for special needs students is not always provided in a public school setting. It can be provided at home, in private school and even in a hospital if circumstances warrant.

Special Education During Home Convalescence

The IDEA requires that schools make educational services available to children receiving special education services and who are home or hospital-bound. This is a common scenario for special needs children with certain disabilities who are frequently hospitalized and then remain at home during their recovery. Different schools have different policies on how they carry out their responsibilities to provide an education in these circumstances. It's important to check with your school.

Typically, schools provide a tutor to bring assignments to the student, help complete the assignments and bring the assignments back to the school. While the educational experience will be different than the student's experience when attending school, the tutor is advised to help the student learn the same material as the students who are not homebound.

When a student is hospitalized, the hospital may agree to the same arrangement. However, some hospitals provide the educational services utilizing their own personnel, in coordination with the school. In any case, the hospital will need to review a copy of the student's IEP and may, with the parent's permission, modify it during the student's hospital stay. In most instances, such a modification would address issues arising from the student's medical issues, such as the student's medication schedule or tendency to tire easily. After discharge, the hospital will share a report on the student's progress with the school, and the team should meet at this time to make any necessary changes to the IEP.

Maggie has a degenerative bone disease, utilizes a wheelchair and is eligible for special education services under the category of OHI. She periodically needs surgery to correct orthopedic issues and while she rarely spends more than a week in the hospital, her home convalescence is often six to eight weeks. Maggie is a sophomore and was taking chemistry, a lab course, prior to her most recent surgery. She was also taking art as an elective. The team recognizes that the tutor cannot provide a lab experience in the home, and it is agreed that Maggie will put chemistry on hold and take it next semester. The team also agrees that the school will contract with a local artist who teaches adult education art, who will work with Maggie on her art class curriculum.

Special Needs for Students in Private or Parochial Schools

There are three categories of children with special needs who are attending private school:

1. Those unilaterally placed by their parents or guardian **subsequent** to being determined as eligible for special education services.

2. Those placed by their school district.

3. Those unilaterally placed by their parents or guardian **prior** to being determined as eligible for special education services.

The IDEA mandates that, for parentally placed students, when either the parent or guardian, or the private school, requests an evaluation of the student to determine eligibility, or seeks an updated assessment of a student already determined to be eligible, it is the responsibility of the local public school district where the private school is located to conduct the assessments.

If a parentally placed student is found to be eligible for special education, the local district may provide special education and related services. However these students are not entitled to FAPE and therefore have fewer rights and protections than those students attending public school. If the student reenrolls in a public school, he or she will be legally entitled to the full range of special education and related services.

Parentally placed private school students who are to receive special education and related services receive an **"Individualized Services Plan (ISP)."** This plan typically provides fewer services, and less protection, than an IEP.

Private School as Only FAPE Option

If you place your child in a private school for the purpose of obtaining what you consider to be a more appropriate education, you can request that the school district pay for the private school placement. However, there are very specific requirements that parents in such a situation must follow. First, the family must provide written notice to the school before removing the student. Next, if the school district refuses cover the private school tuition, the parents must demonstrate to a due process hearing officer that the district is either unable, or unwilling, to provide FAPE.

Some examples of a district's inability or unwillingness to provide a FAPE might include a refusal to provide small group instruction when professionally indicated, medical support for a student with special medical needs or a building which is inaccessible to the special needs student.

Nine-year-old Jimmy suffers from serious anxiety and panic attacks, exacerbated when he is around large groups. He attends a very large school, and there is no possibility of delivering his educational services individually or in a small group setting. The school district argues to the hearing officer that only by being around larger groups of people will Jimmy become acclimated to them. However the hearing officer determines that, at this time, Jimmy needs services that the district is unable to provide, and orders the district to pay the tuition for Jimmy to attend a small Montessori school in the same city, and to pay for all of the services indicated on his IEP as well as transportation to the school.

Sometimes the school district will concede to the IEP team that they are unable to provide FAPE to the student. If the team determines that the student's needs can only be met by a private placement, this becomes part of the student's IEP as developed by the team, and the student is placed in the private placement by the district. Such a placement can be either a day placement or a residential placement, if that is determined to be necessary. These students have the same rights as special needs students in public placement, including the right to FAPE.

Homeschooling Special Needs

The IDEA requires school districts to spend "some" funds on services for students not in public school, including homeschooled students. It does not, however, create an entitlement for such students to receive a certain level of specific services. If you are homeschooling, or plan to homeschool your child with disabilities, you should decide whether certain school district services would enhance your child's education. If yes, you should approach your school district and request an ISP for your child. Participate in the ISP meeting as if your child were enrolled in the school and ask for those services you think would best support your child in making educational progress.

If you plan to homeschool your child, it is advisable to engage a lay advocate, or even an attorney who is familiar with special education law since, as noted above, your child does not have an entitlement to any specific services. However, a positive relationship with the school district will go a long way towards acquiring necessary services for your child. And if you eventually place your child in public school, since that is always your right, it can't hurt to develop a good relationship with the school district.

Discipline for Special Education Students

Special needs education can be tailored to include aids and services for a child with problem behaviors. The IEP team works to address and resolve these issues.

If your child has demonstrated behavioral issues at school, the IEP team must address the issue by developing a **"Behavioral Intervention Plan (BIP)."** A BIP addresses problem behaviors that the student has, or may engage in, and includes positive behavioral interventions, supports and strategies. It may also include program modifications and supplementary aids and services to help address the problem behavior.

An expert in problem behavior is often called into the process, so that the BIP is tailored to the individual student's problem behaviors. Sometimes, a "functional behavioral assessment" will be completed, in order to identify the reasons for a specific behavior and to help the IEP team provide interventions that directly address the problem behavior.

If disciplinary action will last ten days or fewer, a student receiving special education services can receive the same discipline as a non-disabled student in the same circumstances.

If disciplinary action will last more than ten days, such as a lengthy suspension, the IEP team must meet to make two determinations as to whether the conduct was:

1. Caused by, or had a direct and substantial relationship to, the student's disability. This is called a **"manifestation determination."**

2. The direct result of the school's failure to implement the IEP and/or the BIP.

If the manifestation determination finds a direct and substantial relationship, the student is returned to his or her placement, unless the team, including the parents, agrees to a new placement. Likewise, if the behavior was due to the school's failure to implement the IEP and/or the BIP, the student is returned to his or her placement.

Conversely, if the team finds that the behavior was not directly related to the disability, the same disciplinary actions can be imposed on the student with a disability as those imposed on a non-disabled student, including expulsion. However, if students are expelled, they must continue to receive education services that will allow them to progress towards meeting their IEP goals and participate in the general education curriculum, although in a different setting.

A school may request that a hearing officer allow the school to remove a student for up to forty-five school days if the school believes that returning the student to his or her placement is substantially likely to result in injury to the student or to other students.

Alternative Educational Settings

There are certain offenses that can lead to a student receiving special education services in an interim **"alternative educational setting (AES)"** for up to forty-five school days, even if the conduct is found to be related to the student's disability. These offenses include:

- Carrying or possessing a weapon at school, on the way to school, at a school event or on school premises.

- Knowingly possessing or using illegal drugs or selling or soliciting the sale of illegal drugs while at school or a school function.

- Inflicting serious bodily injury upon another person while at school or at a school function.

Under no conditions can a student identified as eligible for special education services lose that eligibility because of behavior issues.

Margot is a sophomore in high school and is receiving special education services for a learning disability. One day at lunch, she throws a plate of food at another student who made a snide comment to her. While her parents argued that this behavior was substantially related to her disability, the team determined that it was not related. Margot was suspended for fifteen days and began receiving her services at the community library.

The school then argued to a hearing officer that Margot should be placed in an AES for forty-five days because of the potential for her to cause bodily injury to another person. The hearing officer, however, found that Margot was not substantially likely to cause such an injury. Since the fifteen days of suspension had passed, Margot was permitted to return to school.

Parents can appeal an AES placement to a hearing officer. The hearing must be held within twenty school days of the request, and the decision must be issued within ten days after the hearing.

Severe Behavior That Prevents School Attendance

If any child's behavior is a danger to themselves or to others in the school setting, placement in a therapeutic school may be required. A team determines the least restrictive alternative that affords the student an opportunity to make educational progress while keeping him or her and others safe.

Therapeutic schools are usually either day schools or residential schools, and they provide therapy and psychiatric supports along with academic services. If this is the only setting within which the student can receive an education, at least at the time, then the school district is required to place the student in a day school placement. If there are no local therapeutic day schools available, or if the student requires more intense intervention, he or she may be placed in a residential setting. The school district is required to pay for the educational cost of such a placement, while your state's Medicaid program will likely pick up the residential and therapeutic portion of the services.

Keep in mind that each state has its own criteria for these placements, so ask the school to either contact the appropriate state agency or give you the information to make the contact.

Therapeutic placements are almost always older children, mostly high school age, and are often temporary. That being said, students with serious behavioral and emotional issues often remain in such placements for a number of years. The goal, however, is always to return the student to the public school.

REAL LIFE EXAMPLE

Tom is 16 years old, has bipolar disorder and oppositional-defiant disorder. He is very unpredictable and has serious problems with anger control. He recently got into an unprovoked fight with another student and broke the student's arm. Under the IDEA, the school is permitted to place him outside of the school. The family engages a psychiatrist to evaluate Tom and submit a report to the team. The psychiatrist recommends placement in a residential placement in another part of the state. The team agrees and directs the special education director to contact the state agency responsible for Medicaid funding. Since Tom is currently very agitated and very unpredictable, the psychiatrist checks him into an acute psychiatric facility. Once the residential funding issues are worked out, the team rewrites Tom's IEP, with input from the psychiatrist, and Tom is transferred to the residential therapeutic facility.

What's Next? Transition Planning

For special needs students, transition planning begins as early as age fourteen to consider what path may be best for the student. Depending on the disability, career development can take many forms.

The IDEA requires that transition planning begin at the earliest appropriate age, sometimes even as early as age fourteen. The IEP team makes the determination of when to begin planning for the future. Once it is decided that it is time to begin transition planning, the IEP must include certain elements, which are dictated by a statement of the student's likely post-secondary course. This path could envision college, community college, adult education, vocational-technical training, other craft training or sheltered employment preparation.

When the team decides to begin transition planning, the first step is to identify annual goals and services that will best prepare your child for the transition to life outside of school. Such services might include enrollment in a career development class to explore various career options, field trips to various businesses, and even shadowing owners or workers at such businesses.

Are Transition IEP Teams Different?

While the transition team should include those individuals who work with, or have information about, the student in the educational setting, as well as any therapists, counselors and other professionals that work with the student, there are some very important additions to the team at this juncture. First and foremost, the student should become a member of the team, if he has not yet been participating. The team should also include:

- Representatives of adult services agencies (e.g., voc-rehab) from which the student might begin receiving services.

- College admissions officer, guidance counselor or a career counselor, as appropriate.

- Representatives of transportation services, if the student will need to access such services to get to training, work or school.

Life Beyond High School: Transition Services

Transition services are based on the student's needs, taking into account his or her preferences, abilities and interests. They can include:

- Instruction.

- Community activities.

- Development of employment and other post-secondary school adult-living objectives.

- Acquisition of daily living skills, financial competency skills and the like.

The IDEA requires that transition services be implemented by age sixteen. However, some states require implementation at age fourteen, so check with your state department of education.

Elements of a Transition IEP

The transition IEP must include a statement of necessary transition services, including a statement of interagency responsibilities, as well as a coordinated set of activities that the student will engage with, and which have measurable outcomes. It must be updated annually, or more frequently. If the student is not progressing towards the desired outcomes, the IEP must be revised by the team.

Once students with disabilities leave high school, they can be considered for adult services. Prior to leaving school, therefore, the IEP transition team should gather data from assessments, testing, medical evaluations, observations and other sources to support a determination of eligibility for adult services.

If your young adult student is interested in further education, encourage that. Colleges, community colleges and vocational-technical schools almost always have an office or department which serves the needs of disabled students. These offices may provide academic counseling, referrals for remedial services such as note takers, study partners, sign language interpreters, classroom aides and homework buddies. They can also facilitate with obtaining Braille and audio text books and other needed services. The support folks are usually other students who are studying to become professionals in the special education field and, because they are in the student's age group, can also provide social support, friendship and a sympathetic ear.

If your young adult is significantly disabled, work with the school and your state's voc-rehab agency to provide the independent living skills that he or she will require. You may also want to think about alternative living arrangements, such as group homes. This is the time to start investigating possibilities and alternatives. While you may assume that your child will always live with you, you need to prepare for the time when your child will live as independently as possible, not in your care.

Mickey, who is seventeen years old, was diagnosed with Asperger's at age six and has been either in special education or receiving accommodations under a 504 plan since that time. His social skills have always been problematic, and he can be very know-it-all and bossy. But in many ways, he does "know it all" when it comes to films. He enters a trivia match and takes home the prize because many of the questions involved films.

Mickey is graduating in a year and the team is implementing his transition plan. Mickey marches into a team meeting, with his award from the contest, and announces that he wants to work in film. The team decides to add some social skills training to his 504 plan, to help him learn how to promote himself without alienating folks. They also convince a local historical film archive to let him shadow the archivist in her job. By the time Mickey graduates, he has had a job offer from the film archives as well as some new friends.

If students are eighteen years old or older, they can invite their parents or guardian to attend an IEP meeting. However the parents or guardian cannot attend if the students object to their attendance.

Concluding Thoughts

Special education law can be a lot to deal with, especially when facing other challenges raising a special needs child. But perseverance can really pay because you will maximize educational opportunities for your child.

Special education law is complicated and dealing with it is frustrating, not only to parents but to attorneys who practice in this field. But the struggle to understand it is worth the effort, because what is more important to parents, and those that support them, than ensuring that children with special challenges are given the opportunity to develop and achieve to the maximum extent possible? All children deserve this opportunity.

Glossary

Alternative Educational Setting (AES): A place, such as a community library, where a student may receive educational services on an interim basis when not permitted to attend school, because of disciplinary or other issues.

Behavioral Intervention Plan (BIP): A BIP addresses problem behaviors that the student has, or may engage in, and includes positive behavioral interventions, supports and strategies.

Due Process Hearing: An administrative hearing presided over by an independent hearing officer, concerning a failed IEP, at which the school district and the parents can offer information and evidence to facilitate a determination.

Early Intervention: Process by which young children, already identified with a physical or mental condition that has a high probability of causing, or having caused, a developmental delay, are provided services.

Extended School Year (ESY): Refers to providing certain services beyond the school year, if regression by the student is anticipated because of summer or school vacations.

Free, Appropriate Public Education (FAPE): The standard used in the context of disabled children and to which all children are entitled by law to receive.

Federal Rehabilitation Act: Law that prevents those receiving federal funding from discriminating against those with disabilities. Mandates "accommodations" for those with disabilities in certain situations including education.

Individuals with Disabilities Education Act (IDEA): Law enacted in 1975 mandating that states provide special education for those with disabilities.

Glossary

IDEA Disabilities: Disabilities covered by IDEA include autism, deafness, deaf-blindness, hearing impairment, mental retardation, multiple disabilities, speech or language impairment, traumatic brain injury, blindness, specific learning disability and a serious emotional disturbance.

Individual Education Plan (IEP): A plan formulated by a school district to address a child's educational needs. It's a road map of sorts to enable a child to make progress.

Individualized Family Service Plan (IFSP): An early intervention plan formulated for a young (preschool age child) to assist with developmental challenges exhibited or anticipated because of the child's needs.

Individualized Services Plan (ISP): This plan is created for a special needs student who has been parentally placed in a private school. This plan typically provides fewer services, and less protection, than an IEP.

Least Restrictive Environment: This mandate requires that Pre-K children, entitled to FAPE, be educated alongside children without disabilities to the maximum extent possible.

Other Health Impaired (OHI): A catchall category that includes disabilities that do not fit into other disabilities categories. These can include things like ADD and ADHD, as well as physical disabilities such as cerebral palsy and spina bifida.

Procedural Safeguards: A statement that lists the family's rights under the IDEA. These include the right to be on the team and get notice of all meetings, provide written consent (or not) to assessments, mediation, a due process hearing and free services.

Statute of Limitations: Law which provides that a lawsuit must be started within a certain period of time, after an incident or the signing of a contract, or else it can longer be brought.

About the Author

Lynne Williams, Esq.

Lynne Williams is a special education attorney who represents families of special needs children at mediation, due process hearings and court proceedings. Lynne has a Ph.D. in social psychology from the University of Southern California and earned her law degree at Golden Gate University School of Law.

Ms. Williams practices law in Maine and is a former Special Education Hearing Officer for the state of Maine. Her son has a disability and it was in her quest to understand special education law that she attended law school. Ms. William urges that in the end, experience, and not law school, proved the better teacher.

About Real Life Legal™

Parker Press Inc., the publisher of Real Life Legal™ creates plain language consumer information on legal, tax, business and financial subjects. Taking aim at info overload and legalese, Parker Press Inc. launched Real Life Legal™ in 2014. Real Life Legal™ provides practical advice, written by lawyers, to help people understand how the law works. Our goal is to provide solid, easy-to-understand information so *you* can decide whether it makes sense to hire a lawyer. Real Life Legal™ wants you to be prepared.

Available Titles

Bankruptcy Basics: Chapter 7 and Chapter 13
Marina Ricci, Esq.

Business Owners Startup Guide
Susan G. Parker, Esq. and Lynne Williams, Esq.

Elder Law: Legal Planning for Seniors
Susan G. Parker, Esq. and Maria B. Whealan, Esq.

Employee's Guide to Discrimination and Termination
Joanne Dekker, Esq.

Estate Planning: A Road Map for Beginners
Susan G. Parker, Esq. and Maria B. Whealan, Esq.

Filing a Homeowner's Claim: Natural Disaster or Not
Dawn Snyder, Esq.

A Lawyer's Guide to Home Renovations
John A. Goodman, Esq.

Available Titles (Continued)

Planning for Pets: Trusts, Leash Laws and More
Joanne Dekker, Esq.

Planning for Your Special Needs Child
Amy Newman, Esq.

Special Needs Education: Navigating for Your Child
Lynne Williams, Esq.

U.S. Veterans: Your Rights and Benefits
Maria B. Whealan, Esq.
with Paul M. Goodson, Esq.

What to Do When Someone Dies
Susan G. Parker, Esq.

You've Been Arrested: Now What?
Maryam Jahedi, Esq.

Notes

Notes

Notes

Notes

Notes

Notes

Notes

Notes

Notes

Notes

Notes

Notes

Notes

Notes

Notes

Notes

Notes

Notes

Notes

www.ingramcontent.com/pod-product-compliance
Lightning Source LLC
Chambersburg PA
CBHW060632210326
41520CB00010B/1566